I0425341

Cursive Penmanship Workbook for Teens

Practice Workbook with a Modern Script Font and Inspiring Quotes that Build a Nuanced Personality in a Young Teenager

Legal & Disclaimer

The information contained in this book and its contents are not designed to replace or take the place of any form of medical or professional advice. The information provided by this book is not meant to replace the need for independent medical, financial, legal or other professional advice or services, as may be required.

The content and information contained in this book have been compiled from sources deemed reliable and are accurate to the best of the Author's knowledge and belief. The Author cannot, however, guarantee its accuracy and validity and cannot be held liable for any errors and/or omissions. When needed, further changes will be periodically made to this book. Where appropriate and/or necessary, you agree and are obligated to consult a professional before using any information in this book.

Upon using the contents and information contained in this book, you agree to hold the Author harmless from and against any damages, costs, and expenses, including any legal fees potentially resulting from the application of any of the information provided by this book. This disclaimer applies to any loss, damages or injury caused by the use and application, whether directly or indirectly, of any advice or information presented, whether for breach of contract, tort, negligence, personal injury, criminal intent, or under any other cause of action.

You agree to accept all risks of using the information presented in this book.

Cursive Penmanship Workbook for Teens: Practice Workbook with a Modern Script Font and Inspiring Quotes that Build a Nuanced Personality in a Young Teenager
Copyright © 2019 by Ellie Roberts
All rights reserved.

Not Your Typical Cursive Handwriting Workbook!

Cursive penmanship has become a lost artform. However, this workbook has set out to revive that artform and combine the standard cursive style with modern calligraphy.

This book, therefore, was not designed to teach standard cursive handwriting, but something a bit more sophisticated. That's why it would be advantageous if you would already possess the skills to write in the standard form of cursive. (If not, we have some great books designed to teach that too!)

So, let's put in simple. What is this workbook really about? Essentially, it's an introduction to a handwriting style with calligraphic elements. This workbook builds upon the traditional handwriting style and allows you to discover an easy way of adding a nuanced touch of calligraphy to your handwriting.

It is designed for beginners and intermediates since it mostly focuses on the cursive writing of entire words and sentences.

This book does, however, contain a short practice section for each letter. This overview also includes recommendations on how each letter should be written. The rest of the workbook contains personal inspiring quotes. The quotes are easy to understand and remember so you can start applying them instantly.

Read the quotes carefully, remember the lessons they teach and try to implement these lessons in your daily life.

In addition, we added a table with a comparison between the *Standard Cursive Style* and the *Modern Script Font* taught in this workbook.

Standard Cursive	*Modern Script Font*
$\mathcal{A}\, a$	$\mathcal{A}\, a$
$\mathcal{B}\, b$	$\mathcal{B}\, b$
$\mathcal{C}\, c$	$\mathcal{C}\, c$
$\mathcal{D}\, d$	$\mathcal{D}\, d$
$\mathcal{E}\, e$	$\mathcal{E}\, e$
$\mathcal{F}\, f$	$\mathcal{F}\, f$
$\mathcal{G}\, g$	$\mathcal{G}\, g$

H h	H h
I i	I i
J j	J j
K k	K k
L l	L l
M m	M m
N n	N n
O o	O o

$P\ p$	$P\ p$
$Q\ q$	$Q\ q$
$R\ r$	$R\ r$
$S\ s$	$S\ s$
$T\ t$	$T\ t$
$U\ u$	$U\ u$
$V\ v$	$V\ v$
$W\ w$	$W\ w$

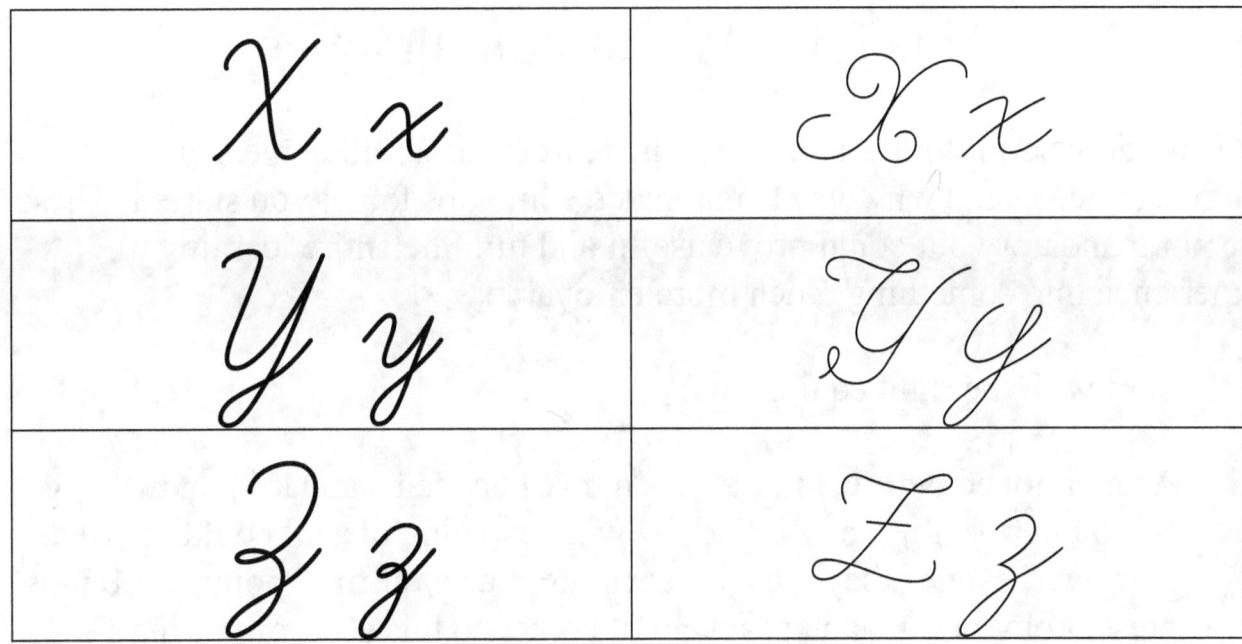

Over time, you can allow this modern script font to evolve naturally and develop into something unique to your personality.

Tips for a Memorable Practice

This modern script font is a bit more difficult to master than the standard cursive style. That's why we also included some tips to get you started. These are not mandatory but could prove useful and turn the entire learning experience into something much more enjoyable:

1. Start with the right equipment

   As mentioned before, this style is a mix between standard handwriting and modern calligraphy. That's why any writing utensil could be used. However, even if they are a bit tricky to master at first, pointed dib nips present obvious advantages when it comes to this style of writing. The pointed sharp nibs allow swirling flourishes and thin strokes to come much more easily.

2. Prepare the workspace

   First, you should clear the table and prepare a clean and organized practice environment.

   Second, you should prepare the supplies: a pen with a pointed dib nip (if you decided to use one), ink, the workbook, and additional paper.

3. Study each letter

   It might be tempting to go directly to the exercises and skip the individual letter practice. However, if you take a little bit of extra time to study and practice each letter, you will find it a lot easier to create a natural flow when writing entire words or sentences. You can even practice each letter on a blank paper to completely familiarize yourself with the motion.

4. Have fun

Remember that for such a style of handwriting to develop easily and evolve naturally, the entire practice must occur with enjoyment and fun. The art of penmanship is something that can offer a unique touch to any written content. The learning experience should, therefore, be done with love so that the same feeling can be seen on paper.

A word of caution: During your practice, you might find it difficult to keep a steady flow during the hardwiring process. It's important to not get frustrated and keep practicing. This handwriting style depends entirely on steady strokes so don't get discouraged if the first few sentences won't be that "good-looking." Remember, over time you will develop a unique handwriting style filled with calligraphic elements which will embellish any written content of yours.

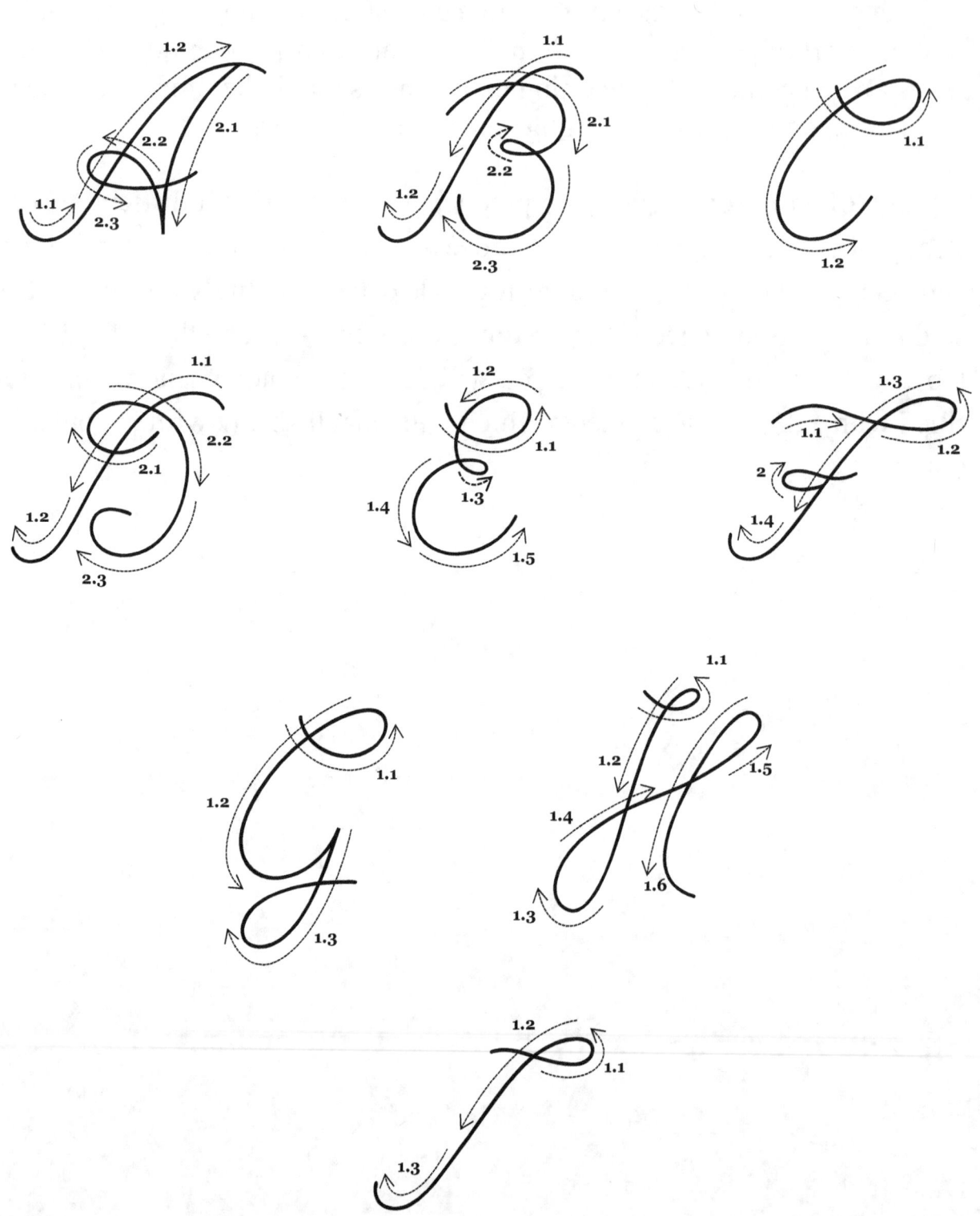

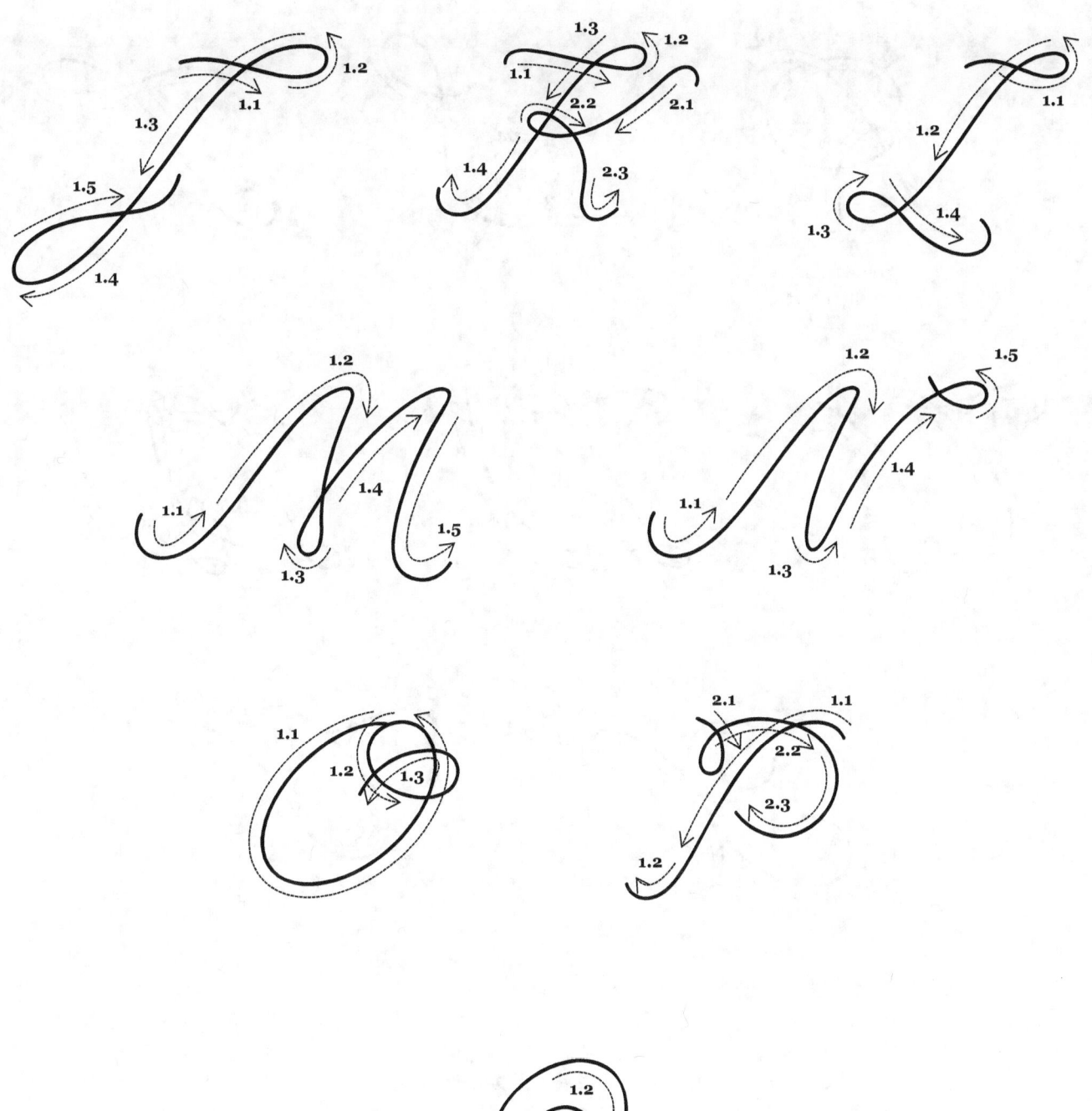

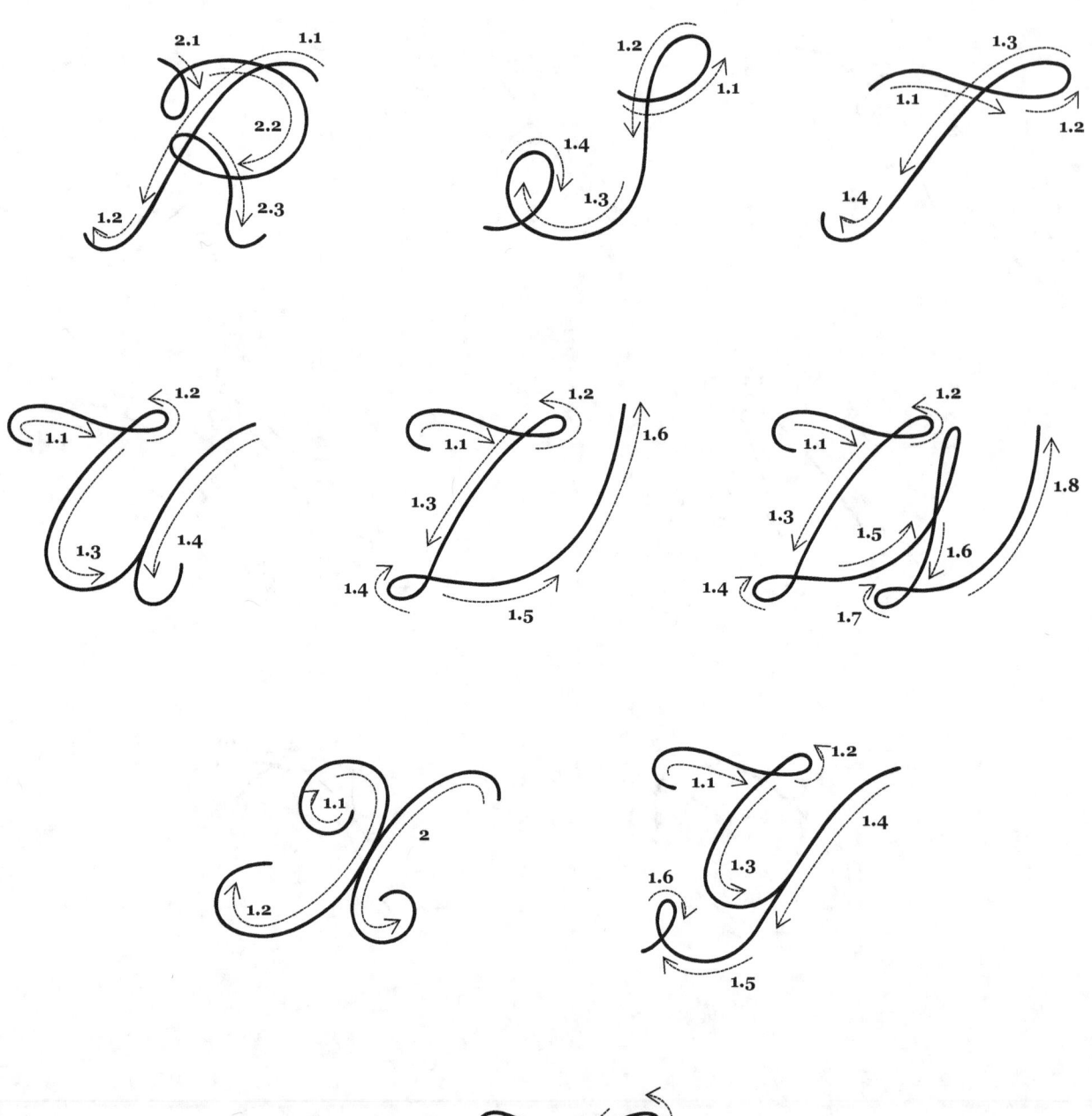

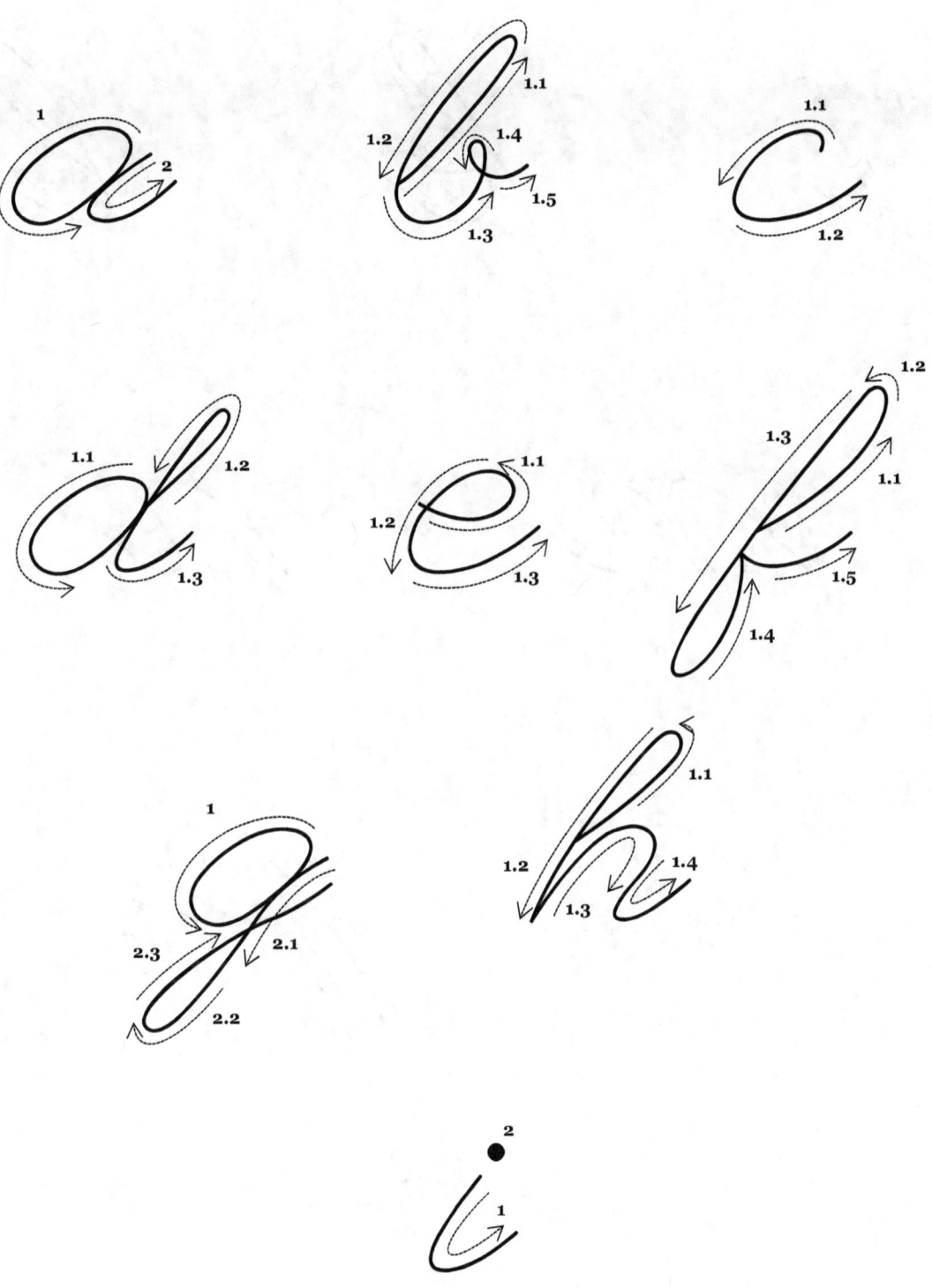

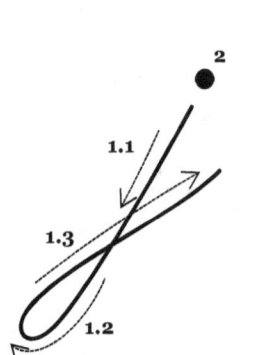

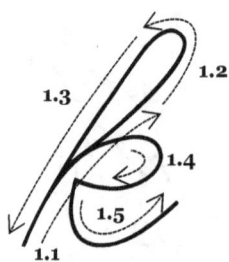

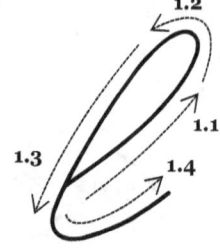

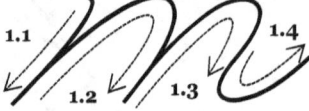

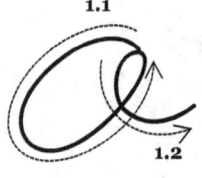

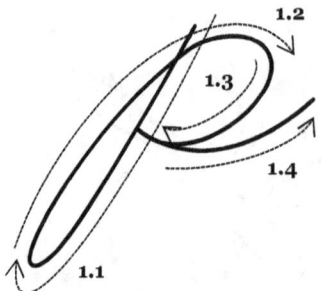

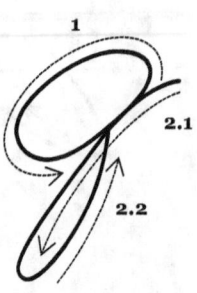

Modern script font - lowercase letters 3/3
(r, s, t, u, v, w, x, y, z)

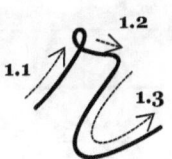
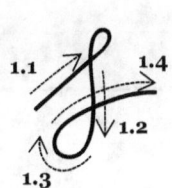
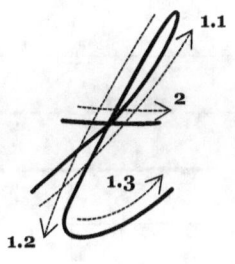

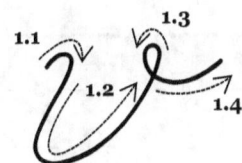
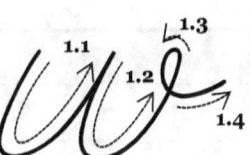

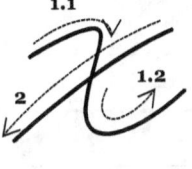
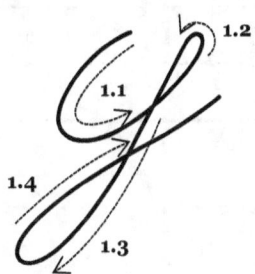

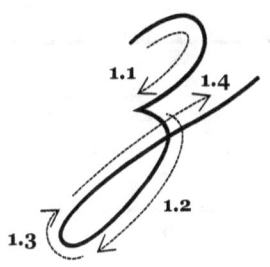

Modern script letter practice

A

a

B

b

C

c

D

d

E

e

F

f

G

g

H

h

I

i

J

j

k

k

L

l

M

m

N

n

O

O

P

R

Q

g

R

r

S

s

T

No matter how sad the day may be,
smile and be grateful for your blessings.

day

smile

grateful

blessings

Copy the entire previous quote below while using your best handwriting.

One small act of kindness each day will keep you filled with joy and happiness all your life.

small

act

filled

life

Copy the entire previous quote below while using your best handwriting.

Never let the opinions of other people keep you from doing what you love.

opinions

other

people

doing

Copy the entire previous quote below while using your best handwriting.

If you love the work you do, you will
always perform at your highest.

work

will

always

perform

Copy the entire previous quote below while using your best handwriting.

If you can't decide on something important, it might be better to take a break and clear your mind.

decide

might

clear

mind

Copy the entire previous quote below while using your best handwriting.

Virtues are habits, so learn them from a young age.

habits

learn

young

age

Copy the entire previous quote below while using your best handwriting.

Quote #7

Knowledge may present us with scary truths, but knowledge also sets us free.

may

scary

sets

free

Copy the entire previous quote below while using your best handwriting.

By deceiving others, you deceive
yourself.

others

you

deceive

yourself

Copy the entire previous quote below while using your best handwriting.

Take a look at your own flaws before
pointing out the flaws of others.

Take

look

before

pointing

Copy the entire previous quote below while using your best handwriting.

Never be afraid to ask "Why?" – no matter how uncomfortable it might seem.

afraid

ask

matter

seem

Copy the entire previous quote below while using your best handwriting.

Don't just be yourself, be the best version
of yourself.

Don't

just

best

version

Copy the entire previous quote below while using your best handwriting.

Remember the lessons of the past, but always live in the present.

lessons

past

always

live

Copy the entire previous quote below while using your best handwriting.

Quote #13

Overthinking can turn the simplest answers into the most complicated riddles.

turn

simplest

most

riddles

Copy the entire previous quote below while using your best handwriting.

Quote #14

Even failure can be a good thing if you keep calm and learn from it.

Even

failure

good

thing

Copy the entire previous quote below while using your best handwriting.

Quote #15

Everyone struggles with challenges.
Empathy allows us to understand and
help each other.

and

help

each

other

Copy the entire previous quote below while using your best handwriting.

If you set out to find something wrong in a person, you might find something, even if it isn't true.

find

you

might

true

Copy the entire previous quote below while using your best handwriting.

Quote #17

No matter how slow your progress, you should always gather the strength to move forward.

matter

slow

move

forward

Copy the entire previous quote below while using your best handwriting.

Quote #18

Always be willing to admit your mistakes and to learn from them.

Always

willing

admit

mistakes

Copy the entire previous quote below while using your best handwriting.

Quote #19

If you want to overcome life's challenges, learn how to keep calm in stressful situations.

want

learn

how

keep

Copy the entire previous quote below while using your best handwriting.

Never judge someone or something that you do not truly understand.

Never

judge

someone

truly

Copy the entire previous quote below while using your best handwriting.

Quote #21

The best way to defeat your foes is to turn them into friends.

way

defeat

foes

friends

Copy the entire previous quote below while using your best handwriting.

If you are capable of doing a good deed,
it's your responsibility to do it.

capable

doing

good

deed

Copy the entire previous quote below while using your best handwriting.

The wisest men know when to trust their heart, but also when to trust their mind.

know

heart

trust

mind

Copy the entire previous quote below while using your best handwriting.

Happiness about the misfortune of
another person is just an illusion.

about

another

just

illusion

Copy the entire previous quote below while using your best handwriting.

The world is beautiful, but most of us never bother to take a look.

world

most

bother

look

Copy the entire previous quote below while using your best handwriting.

Quote #26

Every creature deserves kindness, no matter how small or how different from us it might be.

Every

creature

deserves

kindness

Copy the entire previous quote below while using your best handwriting.

Discipline is the foundation of true greatness.

Discipline

the

true

greatness

Copy the entire previous quote below while using your best handwriting.

Nothing good ever came from laziness.

Nothing

came

from

laziness

Copy the entire previous quote below while using your best handwriting.

Quote #29

True richness doesn't come from the outside, it comes from within.

True

richness

from

within

Copy the entire previous quote below while using your best handwriting.

Quote #30

Every idea is worth considering at least
once, no matter how silly it might seem.

once

silly

might

seem

Copy the entire previous quote below while using your best handwriting.

Great ideas won't befall you if you aren't looking for them.

Great

ideas

befall

looking

Copy the entire previous quote below while using your best handwriting.

Never envy the success of others. Praise
it with honesty and learn from it.

Never

success

others

Praise

Copy the entire previous quote below while using your best handwriting.

Quote #33

Learn how to be alone, and you will never feel lonely.

Learn

alone

will

lonely

Copy the entire previous quote below while using your best handwriting.

Always have an open mind, and accept that you can always learn something new.

open

mind

accept

always

Copy the entire previous quote below while using your best handwriting.

You'll never overcome your fears if you
don't have the courage to face them.

your

courage

face

them

Copy the entire previous quote below while using your best handwriting.

Quote #36

One of the greatest strengths you can
have is knowing how to listen.

One

greatest

strengths

listen

Copy the entire previous quote below while using your best handwriting.

Quote #37

Wisdom comes from knowledge and experience.

comes

from

knowledge

and

Copy the entire previous quote below while using your best handwriting.

A strong mind can overcome any
challenge and solve any problem.

strong

mind

challenge

problem

Copy the entire previous quote below while using your best handwriting.

Learn to focus on the task at hand, no matter how insignificant it might seem.

Learn

focus

task

hand

Copy the entire previous quote below while using your best handwriting.

Quote #40

No matter how hard you fall in life, if you have the strength to get back up, you will never be defeated.

matter

hard

fall

life

Copy the entire previous quote below while using your best handwriting.

Quote #41

The most significant growth always happens outside your comfort zone.

happens

outside

comfort

zone

Copy the entire previous quote below while using your best handwriting.

Quote #42

Treat others with the same respect with which you treat yourself.

Treat

others

with

respect

Copy the entire previous quote below while using your best handwriting.

www.ingramcontent.com/pod-product-compliance
Lightning Source LLC
Chambersburg PA
CBHW081400280526
45788CB00009B/2938